HOMESTEADING ON THE PLAINS

Daily Life in the Land of Laura Ingalls Wilder

MARY DODSON WADE

The Millbrook Press
Brookfield, Connecticut

For Dana, Sally, and 'Nea,
who made those trips with me.
                    M.D.W.

Cover painting by Harvey Dunn courtesy of The South Dakota Art Museum Collection("The Prairie Is My Garden"). Paintings by Harvey Dunn courtesy of The Moody County Public Library: p. 4 ("The First Furrow"); Hazel L. Meyer Memorial Library, De Smet, S.D.: pp. 10 ("In Search of the Land of Milk and Honey"), 18 ("Pioneer Woman"); The South Dakota Art Museum Collection: pp. 16 ("Bringing Home the Bride"), 23 ("Home"), 26 ("Buffalo Bones Are Plowed Under"), 29 ("The Stone Boat"), 36 ("Something for Supper"), 40 ("Homesteader's Wife"), 44 ("After School"), 49 ("School Day's End"), 50 ("Jedediah Smith in the Badlands"), 54 ("Happy Hunting Ground"), 56 ("I Am the Resurrection and the Life"), 62 ("After the Blizzard"), 66 ("Storm Front").

Library of Congress Cataloging-in-Publication Data
Wade, Mary Dodson.
Homesteading on the plains : daily life in the land of Laura Ingalls Wilder / Mary Dodson Wade; with paintings by Harvey Dunn.
p.   cm.
Includes biographical references (p.).
Summary: Quotes from the writings of Laura Ingalls Wilder and paintings by one of her relatives accompany accounts of pioneer life in the Midwest during the second half of the 1800s.
ISBN 0-7613-0218-2 (lib. bdg.)
1. Wilder, Laura Ingalls, 1867–1957—Homes and haunts—Great Plains—Juvenile literature. 2. Women authors, American—20th century—Biography—Juvenile literature. 3. Frontier and pioneer life—Great Plains—Juvenile literature. [1. Frontier and pioneer life—Great Plains. 2. Wilder, Laura Ingalls, 1867–1957—Homes and haunts.] I. Wilder, Laura Ingalls, 1867–1957. II. Dunn, Harvey, 1884–1952, ill.
PS3545.I342Z918   1997 813'.52 [B]—DC21   96-37833   CIP   AC

Published by The Millbrook Press, Inc.
2 Old New Milford Road, Brookfield, Connecticut 06804

CONTENTS

INTRODUCTION

In the latter part of the nineteenth century, thousands of families, lured by land that could be theirs almost free of charge, left good homes in the eastern part of the United States for an uncertain future in the west. Children, because of choices made by their parents, suddenly faced a very different life.

Sometimes they had cousins, aunts, uncles, and grandparents nearby when whole families moved together. Sometimes neighbors from one place moved and settled near each other. But it was more common for single families to sell everything and head west. In some cases the man went first and sent for his family later, but whatever the arrangement, the family faced a different set of circumstances in the west.

Charles Ingalls was typical of a man who moved his family into the great grasslands of the prairies and plains during the 1870s and 1880s. In his daughter Laura's "Little House" books, readers follow the Ingallses on a long, zigzag journey.

In 1867, Laura was born to Caroline and Charles Ingalls in the *Little House in the Big Woods*, near Pepin, Wisconsin. She and her sister Mary, who was two years older, had lots of cousins living near them.

By 1869, however, they were on their way to Montgomery County, Kansas, where Charles Ingalls built a log cabin on Indian land, believing that it was open for settlement. In 1870, a third sister, Carrie, was born in the *Little House on the Prairie*, but the Ingallses soon returned to their Wisconsin farm. Not only was there a problem in getting title to the Indian land, but the man who had bought the Ingalls's Wisconsin farm had not paid for it.

Laura's books do not mention their return to Wisconsin, but records show that Mary and Laura attended school about a mile from their house, and the stories told in *Little House in the Big Woods* are from memories of this period.

Three years later, the Ingallses left the security of nearby relatives a second time and traveled west to Walnut Grove, Minnesota. Their first home *On the Banks of Plum Creek* was a dugout, but they soon built a house of sawed lumber. When grasshoppers ate their crops the next year, they moved into town where Charles Ingalls could get work. Although the Ingallses were still listed as the homesteaders of the Plum Creek property, they never lived there again.

None of Laura's books mention the sad period that followed. Their little brother Freddie, born in 1875 in Walnut Grove, died the following summer at the home of relatives in southeastern Minnesota. The Ingallses were on their way to run a hotel in Burr Oak, Iowa, where a fourth daughter, Grace, was born in 1877.

Returning to Walnut Grove, the Ingallses lived in town for a year before making their last move westward when Charles Ingalls took a job as timekeeper and storekeeper for the railroad. In Dakota Territory they lived *By the Shores of Silver Lake*. Until a newly married couple, Mr. and Mrs. Boast, arrived to help them celebrate a mild New Year's Day 1880, they were the only people at the place that became De Smet, South Dakota.

The following year they spent *The Long Winter* in a building that Charles Ingalls had constructed on the main street. He probably would have moved west again, but his wife, Caroline, resisted the idea. In *Little Town on the Prairie,* her girls were able to go to school.

It was in De Smet that Laura Ingalls met Almanzo Wilder, called Manly by his family. She recorded their courtship and marriage in *These Happy Golden Years*.

Many years after Laura and Almanzo had died, an unfinished manuscript was published. *The First Four Years* describes the tragedies that came to the young couple and how they left South Dakota. *On the Way Home* is Laura's diary of a trip with their little daughter Rose to their new home near Mansfield, Missouri.

Laura Ingalls Wilder grew up familiar with the plains. That is also the place where artist Harvey Dunn was born and the place that inspired much of his art.

Dunn, the nephew of Laura Ingalls Wilder's sister, Grace Ingalls Dow, was born in 1884. This talented son of a South Dakota pioneer family moved east and studied with the noted artist Howard Pyle. As Dunn became better known, his work appeared on the cover of *The Saturday Evening Post*. During World War I, at the age of thirty-four, Dunn was one of eight illustrators chosen to depict the American Army at war. Many of those pictures are in the Smithsonian Institution in Washington, D.C.

Dunn's art studio was in New Jersey, but he enjoyed returning to South Dakota and began to paint scenes from his childhood. In 1950, after being invited to display some of his paintings during "Old Settler's Days" in De Smet, he arrived with forty-two canvases. When the celebration was over, he donated them to the people of his home state. The South Dakota Art Museum on the campus of South Dakota State University in Brookings now holds ninety pieces of his work.

Dunn's paintings are crystal clear in their depiction, but he hated to assign titles. "Madam," he once remarked to a patron, "if you need a title to know what that picture is all about, *I have failed*."

The art in this book is by a native son. The quotations also come from those who lived on the prairie during this time of great challenge.

Laura's experiences were fairly typical of what happened to homesteaders—both good and bad. Her family lived in four widely separated places within a period of ten years, covering 2,000 miles (3,200 kilometers) in their travels. Only the distance was unusual because most homesteaders came from neighboring states.

Moving was one way of dealing with calamities. Laura and Almanzo Wilder left South Dakota. After losing everything due to a drought, they chose to return to an area where more abundant rainfall promised better times.

Although many settlers left, those who stayed turned the grasslands into farms and ranches. Nature in that area is still just as awe-inspiring and unforgiving. A child living on the high plains a century after Laura's experiences described it as "a place where angels drown."

Chapter One

IN SEARCH OF THE LAND OF MILK AND HONEY

"Well, girls, I've bet Uncle Sam fourteen dollars against a hundred and sixty acres of land, that we can make out to live on the claim for five years. Going to help me win the bet?"

"Oh, yes, Pa!" Carrie said eagerly, and Mary said, "Yes, Pa!" gladly, and Laura promised soberly, "Yes, Pa."[1]

By the Shores of Silver Lake

In the half-century following the American Revolution, the edge of the frontier crept westward until it reached the Mississippi River. Then it seemed to stop. Even though the United States doubled its territory when it acquired land west of the Mississippi with the Louisiana Purchase in 1803, little was changed other than the flag that flew over the area.

It was the discovery of gold in California in 1848 that sent adventurers rushing headlong across the great river. But they were looking for quick riches on the west coast and completely ignored middle America. Neither they nor the farmers heading to Oregon thought of stopping on the flat, grassy plains.

Perhaps they agreed with Major Stephen Long, who thirty years earlier had led an expedition to the Rocky Mountains. His report included a map that called this area the Great Desert. He concluded:

> In regard to this extensive section of country, we do not hesitate in giving the opinion, that it is almost wholly unfit for cultivation, and of course uninhabitable by a people depending upon agriculture for their subsistence. Although tracts of fertile land, considerably extensive, are occasionally to be met with, yet the scarcity of wood and water, almost uniformly prevalent, will prove an insuperable obstacle in the way of settling the country.[2]

The grasslands stretched hundreds of miles in all directions, but they were not empty. Various American Indian tribes roamed the area and lived off animals that thrived there, such as bison and antelope.

By the mid-1860s, however, settlers began to push into the region. Many had lost everything during the Civil War and came west to start again. Not being familiar with the climate, they expected to use the same methods of farming that had worked so well in the east. Through great trial they found this was not possible.

They were encouraged by lenient government land policies. In 1841, Congress had passed the Pre-Emption Act, which gave settlers the right to buy public land for $1.25 an acre. Then came the Homestead Act of 1862, which provided land to settlers for almost no money.

The Homestead Act allowed heads of households, whether citizens or aliens, to file a claim. They had to be twenty-one years of age and could not have borne arms against the United States—a restriction against Confederate soldiers that was removed four years later. By paying a ten-dollar filing fee and other small commissions, the homesteader could claim 160 acres (65 hectares) of land. After building a house and living on the land for five years, settlers "proved up" (showed that they had met the requirements, including citizenship), and the land was theirs.

The method of identifying boundaries of property located in the area west of the original states had been worked out in 1785 when Congress began granting public land to Revolutionary War veterans. Starting at the western boundary of Pennsylvania, the land was marked off into squares identified by a set of three numbers. The first number designated the section, the second the township, and the third the range.

A section was 1 square mile (2.6 square kilometers) and contained 640 acres (260 hectares). Under the Homestead Act, a claim was one-fourth of a section, or 160 acres. The claim was identified as either the NW (northwest), SW (southwest), NE (northeast), or SE (southeast) quarter of a certain section. Today, section-line roads in the middle of the country run arrow-straight with right-angle turns as they give access to all quarters of a section.

Thirty-six adjoining sections made a township, which was also assigned a number. For the purpose of government, the townships were given names. Later, as more settlers came to an area, they formed villages within the township or even across township lines. Township names are almost forgotten today, but census takers of that time used these names as they recorded residents.

The third number for a claim designated the range. Range was based on longitude, the imaginary lines running between the North and South Poles that tell the distance east or west of Greenwich, England. The farther west a place was, the higher the range number for a claim.

These three numbers still serve as the legal description of property that lies outside city limits. For example, the farm that Charles Ingalls homesteaded on Plum Creek just north of Walnut Grove, Minnesota, is identified as the NW quarter of Section 18, Township 109, Range 38.

Because the Pre-Emption Act was not repealed until 1891, both pre-emption and homesteading were available to a settler for a while. Laura indicated that her father bargained for their Minnesota property, but the man he bargained with, "Mr. Hanson," did not have legal ownership of the land. Perhaps the Ingallses paid him for the dugout house he had built. Whatever the arrangement, the first name listed on the deed to the property is that of Charles Ingalls, who paid $430.18 for it on July 10, 1876. This deed was a pre-emption patent, taken out three years after the Ingallses came to Walnut Grove. The price was $2.50 rather than $1.25 an acre because the 172-acre (70-hectare) farm was near the railroad.

The same day the Ingallses paid for the farm, they sold it to Abraham and Margaret Keller for $400. The pre-emption method of ownership allowed the Ingalls to have title immediately, so they could sell the place and be on their way to Dakota Territory. Moving before "proving up" was common. Sometimes it was the death of family members, but homesickness and natural disasters also caused settlers to leave. Sometimes it was restlessness and a desire to keep moving. The Ingallses headed west in 1879 because Charles Ingalls had a new job.

Ten years had passed since the big ceremony in Utah, where officials drove a golden spike to complete the first railroad track to run across the continent. Now, smaller companies were furiously laying shorter, connecting tracks across the plains.

The Ingallses left Walnut Grove and accompanied the Chicago and North-Western Railroad as it pushed west from Tracy, Minnesota. The crew reached 25 miles (40 kilometers) into Dakota Territory before workers left for the winter, but the Ingallses stayed in the surveyor's house to take care of railroad tools.

The next year the line was completed to Pierre, 185 miles (298 kilometers) farther west, but the family did not go. That spring Charles

Ingalls filed a homestead claim south of De Smet for the NE quarter of Section 3, Township 110, Range 56.

On the plains, this system of property identification, as precise as it was, still took some ingenuity to figure out. In timbered areas, there was a "witness" tree that bore the stated numbers, but before surveyors arrived to mark the boundaries on the grasslands, settlers had to rely on knowledge of the distance to a claim.

Wagons had no odometers to record mileage as cars do today, but by tying a rag around a spoke and counting the number of revolutions the wheel made, a person knew when a mile had been traveled. Using this method, a family went forth, their wagon tracks lost in a sea of grass. They were headed to a new home.

FLOWERS

Eleven-year-old Lucy Carruth arrived in eastern Kansas in 1856 with her father, mother, and three younger brothers. She sent a letter to her friend in Watertown, New York, soon after their arrival.

Our Tent, Osawatomie, June 1 1856

Dear Fannie:

We arrived at Osawatomie Monday noon; . . . We stayed there a week, during which time father picked out a "claim," and we are now on it. I think it is a beautiful one.

I should like to have you give me a balloon visit. What would you think of flowers up to your neck! Here is spider-wort, phlox, prairie pea, wild verbena (a most beautiful flower), scarlet milk-weed, roses (as many as you could wish), and a great many others that I do not know the names of. I shall save many kinds of seeds this fall. We have a great deal of fruit on our claim— gooseberries, grapes, plums, mulberries, raspberries and others. We have goose-berries every meal. Father has been making garden today; he has peas and beans planted, and a few potatoes that we brought along with us for seed. . . . Mother and I have been to cut some dry prairie-grass to make some beds.[3]

Chapter Two

THE PRAIRIE IS MY GARDEN

Laura went under those singing flowers into the dugout. It was one room, all white. The earth walls had been smoothed and white-washed. The earth floor was smooth and hard....

The front wall was built of sod. Mr. Hanson had dug out his house, and then he had cut long strips of prairie sod and laid them on top of another. . . .

Ma was pleased. She said, "It's small, but it's clean and pleasant." . . .

They all went up the path and stood on the roof of that house. . . .

"Goodness," said Ma. "Anybody could walk over this house and never know it's here."[4]

On the Banks of Plum Creek

Once on their claims, settlers began building a house. While this was being done, the wagon or a brush lean-to served as home. Sometimes they constructed a rough shanty to live in during the growing season. This filled the requirement of living in a house on the property for five months each year. When winter came, some homesteaders retreated to warmer houses in the east until better weather returned.

If the claim was on a creek, the trees there might provide enough timber to build a house. Likewise, if the railroad was nearby and they could afford the cost, homesteaders purchased sawed lumber to make board-and-batten houses, with the cracks between the upright planks covered with narrow strips of wood. Sometimes these houses included a second story.

When no trees were available, settlers used what they had in abundance—a mat of grass and dirt called sod. It was free for a lot of hard work. Long, straight strips of the matted grass, about 2 inches (5 centimeters) thick, were cut with a special plow. The strips were then chopped into "bricks," and the sod was stacked in an overlapping fashion the way bricks are laid.

One form of house was a dugout, which was essentially a cave burrowed into a small rise of land or the high bank of a creek. Dugouts, usually a single room 10 to 12 feet (3 to 3.7 meters) square, had three sides made of dirt and the fourth closed up with sod.

In areas where the land was completely flat, all four walls of the house were made of sod. This house often had several rooms. In some instances, a half-dugout was made by digging a pit several feet deep and surrounding it with sod walls the rest of the way up.

The advantages of a sod house came from its thick, insulating walls. The house was cool in the summer and easy to heat in the winter. Wind didn't whistle through chinks as it did in a log cabin. And sod houses were pretty much fireproof.

For the cash-strapped settlers, the biggest advantage was the cost. There was little to buy beyond a stovepipe, perhaps some lumber, and a few nails.

Howard Ruede, writing home in April 1877, gave an account of the cost of his house:

> I made out an estimate of the cost of our house. . . . Ridge-pole and hauling (including two loads of firewood), $1.50; rafter and straw, 50¢; 2 lb nails, 15¢; hinges, 20¢; window, 75¢; total cash paid, $4.05. Then there was $4 worth of lumber, which was paid for in work, and $1.50 for hauling it over, which, together with hauling the firewood, 50¢, make $10.05 for a place to live in and firewood enough to last all summer.[5]

Living in these houses had definite disadvantages. The sod needed constant repair. Rain washed it away, and water seeped through the roof leaving housewives to cook standing under an umbrella. One settler told of putting the cradle under the table so that the baby would not get rained on.

Dirt also drifted down. And with it came spiders and bugs, even snakes. Bedbugs and fleas were constant annoyances. A cow wandering overhead sometimes punched through the roof.

Fuel to heat the house and cook the food came from buffalo and cow chips. Children had the task of gathering these dried droppings. Coal was used when it could be obtained, but cornstalks, corncobs, and twisted hay also served as fuel.

Housewives made efforts to bring comforts to the house. They cleaned the hardpacked dirt floors with a brush broom and controlled bugs by sprinkling coal oil and water around the room. Sometimes they spread a plaster of sand and clay over the walls to hold the dust in check, and when it was whitewashed, the room was much lighter.

The little furniture they had filled the room. A cookstove stood in the corner, and beds with cornshuck mattresses lined the walls. There might be antique heirlooms, but chairs and tables were often handmade. Some homesteaders, sitting for family pictures outside their sod houses, brought out bedsteads and rocking chairs to show they had real furniture.

Colorful quilts brightened the rooms, and curtains hung at the windows. Some homes even had caged birds to provide a semblance of what the settlers had left far behind.

And no matter how cold the winter, when spring came, flowers bloomed on the roof.

BUILDING
A SOD HOUSE

Howard Ruede, a bachelor living in Kansas in 1877, wrote home describing how a sod house is built.

At Snyder's, Kill Creek, Kansas
Tuesday, March 27, 1877

Perhaps you would be interested in the way a sod house is built. Sod is the most available material, in fact, the only material the homesteader has at hand, unless he happens to be one of the fortunates who secured a creek claim with timber suitable for house logs. Occasionally a new comer has a "bee," and the neighbors for miles around gather at his claim and put up his house in a day. Of course there is no charge for labor in such cases. The women come too, and while the men lay up the sod wall, they prepare dinner for the crowd. . . .

The builder usually "cords up" the sods, though sometimes he crosses the layers, making the walls about two feet thick. . . . When the prairie is thoroughly soaked by rain or snow is the best time for breaking sod for building. The regulation thickness is 2½ inches, buffalo [grass] sod preferred on account of its superior toughness. The furrow slices are laid flat. . . . These furrow slices, 12 inches wide, are cut with a sharp spade into 18-inch lengths, and carefully handled as they are laid in the wall, one length reaching across the wall, which rises rapidly even when the builders are green hands. Care must be taken to break joints and bind the corners of the house. . . . The door and window frames are set in place first and the wall built around them. Building such a house is hard work.

When the square is reached, the crotches (forks of a tree) are set at the ends and in the middle of the house and the ridge pole—usually a single tree trunk the length of the building, but sometimes spliced—is raised to its place by sheer strength of arm, it being impossible to use any other power. Then rails are laid from the ridge log to the walls and covered with any available materials—straight sorghum stalks, willow switches and straw, or anything that will prevent the sod on the roof from falling between the rafters. From the comb of the roof to the earthen floor is usually about nine feet.

The gables are finished before the roof is put on. . . . If the builder is able, he has sawed cottonwood rafters and a pine or cottonwood board roof covered with sod. Occasionally a sod house with a shingle roof is seen, but of course this costs more money.

At first these sod houses are unplastered, and this is thought perfectly all right, but such a house is somewhat cold in the winter, as the crevices between the sods admit some cold air; so some of the houses are plastered with a kind of "native lime," made of sand and a very sticky native clay. This plaster is very good unless it happens to get wet. In a few of the houses this plaster is whitewashed, and this helps the looks very much. Some sod houses are mighty comfortable places to go into in cold weather, and it don't take much fire to keep them warm.[6]

Chapter Three

BUFFALO BONES ARE PLOWED UNDER

From the top of their house, they could see Pa ploughing. The oxen and the plough and Pa crawled slowly along a curve of the prairie. They looked very small, and a little smoke of dust blew away from the plough.

Every day the velvety brown-dark patch of ploughed land grew bigger. It ate up the silvery-gold stubble field beyond the hay-stacks. It spread over the prairie waves. It was going to be a very big wheat-field, and when some day Pa cut the wheat, he and Ma and Laura and Mary would have everything they could think of.

They would have a house, and horses, and candy every day, when Pa made a wheat crop.[7]

On the Banks of Plum Creek

The prairies start abruptly. The eastern part near the Mississippi River is well-watered. Homesteaders there encountered head-high grass. Today, the area extending from Illinois into Iowa is a major corn-producing area of the world.

Charles Ingalls's Wisconsin farm, however, was farther north in the big woods, a belt of timber that stretched into northern Minnesota and spawned the legend of Paul Bunyan. Following tradition, Charles Ingalls cut trees, built a log cabin, and helped turn the Wisconsin countryside into beautiful farmland.

When the Ingallses left that farm, they entered the prairie plains of southern Minnesota. Waist-high grass stretched as far as the eye could see in any direction, and trees grew only along creeks.

Having no trees seemed to mean less work. One observer remarked, "God has cleared the fields." But settlers soon learned that the grass was no ordinary covering. For centuries it had grown, died, and reappeared the following year. The mat was so thick that an ordinary plow was useless.

Horses were not strong enough to break the sod, so the work fell to oxen. To Laura's sorrow, their horses, Pet and Patty, were replaced by big oxen named Pete and Bright. Her father had become a "sodbuster."

When they reached Kingsbury County, South Dakota, however, the Ingallses were just east of the true plains. From the 98th meridian westward to the Rockies, rainfall becomes less and less until it reaches 10 inches (25 centimeters) a year, too dry for farming. This invisible line begins at the Missouri River in the Dakotas. It travels south, splitting

Nebraska and Kansas into two sections, continues through the western part of Oklahoma, and ends in central Texas. Short bunchgrasses such as grama and buffalo grass survive the wind and scant rainfall, but it may take 30 to 50 acres (16 to 20 hectares) of land to provide enough grass for one cow to graze. Ranches there today may cover 50,000 acres (20,235 hectares).

The Ingallses, however, were east of the Missouri River, and grass was still 2 feet (5 meters) high, although rainfall was less than in Minnesota. To be successful, farmers had to change the methods they used.

In areas of little rainfall, it is possible to raise crops by a method called dry farming. This makes use of all available moisture. Hopi Indians have grown corn on their very dry mesas in Arizona for more than a thousand years. They clump plants together and let the searing wind and heat kill the outer shocks, but the protected inner ones yield a harvest. Modern cotton farmers in west Texas plant two rows and skip the third, leaving moisture from the vacant row available for the other two.

The tremendous wheat production of today's upper Midwest makes it the breadbasket for the nation. The wheat thrives in hot summers and cold winters, and the most successful varieties were brought from the "old country" by the waves of Russian immigrants who came to take advantage of the opportunity to own land in America.

Oddly enough, the Homestead Act, which was meant to relieve economic problems for Americans, allowed immigrants from any nation to file for homesteads. One-third of the total population in the Dakotas in 1890 was foreign-born.

The railroads were even more responsible for bringing in settlers. Twice as much land was sold by the railroad companies as was ever homesteaded. The companies received enormous amounts of land as reward for laying track. Blocks of land extending back 10 miles (16 kilometers) or more from the railroad right-of-way were laid out in checkerboard fashion. Every other one belonged to the railroad. Taken together, the area would have been the size of the state of Texas.

Agents went to Europe to hawk railroad land. Advertisements flooded both sides of the Atlantic. The Sioux City and Pacific Railroad proclaimed: FREE HOMES FOR THE MILLIONS. General passenger agent John Ross Buchanan remarked: "It headed every circular, folder, and poster I ever issued, and I issued them by the millions. . . . [i]n every possible publication, in black, blue, and red ink, in English and German." Agents who spoke Swedish, Norwegian, and German were sent to greet immigrants arriving on ships on the east coast.

The terms of a railroad purchase were easy, but not exactly free. After putting one-tenth down, the purchaser had eleven years to pay the rest at 6 or 7 percent interest. During the first three years, a settler could make the first payment and then pay only the interest. There were discounts for paying cash or taking a shorter time to pay. The purchaser's railroad ticket often could be applied to the sale price, and his family and livestock were transported free. Some railroads even furnished seed for planting.

It was good business for the railroads. They received money for land that had cost them nothing except for laying the track, and the settlers became their customers when they shipped their produce.

IMMIGRANTS

In 1898, Jacob Dolwig, his wife, and three children left Hungary and immigrated to Dickinson, North Dakota. After a three-week journey, they stepped off the train into knee-deep snow, not knowing a word of English. The friend who was to meet them was not there.

On February 26, 1898, five o'clock in the morning, we left the village of Tolvadia, Banat, Hungary. . . . Numbers of friends and neighbors followed us to the railway station. . . .

March the first, marked our arrival at Bremen, Germany. . . .

Then we embarked in the steamer, *Dresden*, for our journey to the United States. . . .

March fifteenth—Thirteenth day.

In the morning at ten o'clock we disembarked at Baltimore and caught our first close glimpse of the new land. . . .

There we were registered, giving our age, occupation, religion, and property. . . . There were about three hundred of us there. We bought our tickets to Dickinson, North Dakota. . . .

We traveled all night and the next day. . . . Wonderful growths of wheat were all around us as we traveled, but the surface still consisted of mountains and forests, which disappointed us for we were interested in level land. . . .

We left Chicago March seventeenth. . . .

Some of our fellow passengers left us at Hebron, . . . Taylor and . . . Gladstone. . . .

Suddenly we heard the call "Dickinson," which meant we were at the end of our journey. It was seven o'clock in the morning [March nineteen]. . . . We sank into the snow up to our knees, as we stepped off the train. It was extremely cold. I walked back and forth on the station platform. . . . When I observed the children trembling with cold and fright I became worried and discouraged for the first time during the entire journey, because I realized that I was in a strange land, where a strange language was spoken. There was no one with whom I could speak. The friend, who had written me to come, was not there. The children began to complain about the cold, weariness, and fatigue from the three weeks' travels.

As I looked around, a man approached and asked me in German, "Whom are you looking for? You are an immigrant?"

I answered in the affirmative. I asked him whether he knew a friend of mine J— G—, whom I wired to meet me.

He said, "Yes, I know him, but he cannot come to town because it snowed so much Thursday that the roads are impassable. If you like you can stay with me until he comes."

I asked him whether he had room for all of us.

He answered, "Yes, I will make room, because I, too, was glad when someone sheltered me when I came over from the old country."[8]

Immigrants responded in great numbers. The Dakotas became home to people from Norway, Sweden, Germany, Russia, Switzerland, Belgium, and England. There also were Scotch-Canadians, Jews, and Irish settlers. German Mennonites, a religious group, arrived in Kansas in 1874 with $250,000 in gold, for which the railroad gave them 60,000 acres (24,280 hectares) of land and built barracks for them to use until their houses were ready.

Not only were foreigners allowed to file claims, but women could too, although the constitutional amendment allowing them to vote would not be passed until sixty years after the Homestead Act. Teacher Eliza Jane Wilder was homesteading near De Smet at the same time as her brothers, Royal and Almanzo.

Elizabeth Corey, another woman homesteader, signed stacks of letters to her family back in Iowa as "Bachelor Bess." At her homestead on the Bad River about 10 miles (16 kilometers) southwest of Pierre, South Dakota, she fought heat, blizzards, and rattlesnakes, but managed to attend an occasional social. She taught school to supplement her income. Her brother Fuller often did not agree with her. With pride she noted in 1911 that he "at last told someone that he thought it a wonder that I, a girl alone among strangers, had done so well—better than most of the men had done."

Regardless of who the settler was, the land had to provide food for the family. It was not unusual for homesteaders to arrive in the spring, spend the summer breaking sod on a portion of the farm, then leave for the winter. The following spring they returned and plowed again, sometimes turning over bones of buffalo that had once roamed the plains in great herds.

Those unable to plow their claims hired it done at a cost of three dollars an acre. Men without teams often worked for someone in exchange for help plowing their own fields.

Young children contributed by carrying water or lunch to those working in the fields. And everyone helped at harvest time. The land was the source of life, and the whole family was involved in working it.

Chapter Four

SOMETHING FOR SUPPER

She beat at the birds with her sunbonnet. They rose up swirling on noisy wings and settled again to the corn. . . . They swung clinging to the ears, ripping away the husks, swallowing the corn crop. . . .

[Pa] took his shotgun to the cornfield. . . . Every shot brought down a hail of dead birds. . . . When he had shot away all his cartridges, the swirl of wings seemed no thinner. . . .

When Laura looked for the blackbirds, to dress them for dinner, she could not find them. . . .

"Comb your hair and sit up to the table, Charles," Ma said.

She opened the oven door, and took out the tin milk pan. It was full of something covered thickly over with delicately browned biscuit crust. She set it before Pa and he looked at it amazed. "Chicken pie!"

" 'Sing a song of sixpence—' "said Ma.

Laura went on from there, and so did Carrie and Mary and even Grace.

A pocket full of rye,
Four and twenty blackbirds,
baked in a pie! . . .

"It takes you to think up a chicken pie, a year before there's chickens to make it with," Pa said.[9]

Little Town on the Prairie

With neighbors perhaps a mile or more away and stores even farther, homesteaders had to be self-sufficient. Trips to town were rare, exciting events. Perhaps there would be money enough to buy some calico for a new dress, but more often it went for things the homesteader could not produce—coffee, salt, and molasses. When there was no money or no way to get to town, the settler dreamed up a substitute or did without.

Towns sprang up all along the railroads at designated sites. These towns became market centers, and land near them cost more. Even with pre-emption, homesteaders paid double the price if they chose land near the railroad.

In an experience duplicated many times along the railroad line, the Ingallses watched De Smet's one-story buildings with fake fronts rise on either side of the main street. There were stores, a bank, a post office, and soon a newspaper. Charles Ingalls used his carpentry skills to build two of the first buildings in the center of town. The family survived the long, snowbound winter of 1880–1881 in one of them.

It was the homestead, though, that had to be maintained. Water was the first concern of those who lived there. In Minnesota the Ingallses were lucky enough to have a spring and small stream beside the front door of the dugout. Children often got the job of carrying water. Where there were no streams, wells were dug. In places of adequate rainfall, these were some 20 feet (6 meters) deep, hand-dug, and lined with stones.

For deeper wells an auger drilled down 50 to 100 feet (15 to 30 meters), maybe more. The well had to reach the water table. Hand pumps brought up the water, but windmills soon dotted the landscape bringing water to people and livestock. If the well went dry—which sometimes happened during severe drought—the family was forced to leave.

Small game for food was plentiful at first. The buffalo, which American Indians used for food, clothing, and shelter, had been depleted by 1875; but antelope thrived in the open spaces. Rabbits and turkeys were abundant. Because some animals, like jack rabbits and gophers, were destructive to crops, bounties were placed on them. Children earned money for bringing in their ears or tails. Wolves were considered a menace, and adults shot them to collect bounties for their pelts.

Since the Midwest is on the flyway for migrating birds, ducks and geese were plentiful. Prairie chickens were so numerous that a couple from Fargo returned home from a drive in the spring of 1871 with the wheels of their wagon dripping with egg yolks from the nests they had run over.

Sometimes domesticated chickens came on the train when settlers moved, but usually these were purchased after the family had settled into their new home. Poultry furnished food, and the eggs were sold. Many a housewife got a new dress with her "egg money."

Regardless of what cash crop he raised, every farmer had a garden near the house. It yielded fresh greens, potatoes, turnips, beets, and even okra. The length of the growing season dictated what crops were planted. They had to mature before frost came.

Corn was grown both to eat and to sell. Children turned the coffee mill to grind dried kernels into cornmeal. This was made into cornbread and any number of dishes. White-flour biscuits, a staple of "farm breakfasts" offered in restaurants today, were rare. White flour was so scarce that anything baked with it was considered a dessert.

Even after raising a good crop, the homesteader might lose it to forces over which he had no control. Caroline Ingalls turned the blackbirds that devoured their corn crop into a feast, but grasshoppers did not offer that option. The grasshopper plagues of 1873 and 1874 stretched from Kansas to Minnesota. Grasshoppers stripped everything, even chewing onions and turnips into the ground. They chewed tool handles and even ate the curtains hanging in the windows.

Even if no such tragedy occurred, food was often monotonous because there was little variety, and it did not provide a balanced diet. If things went well, there might be a better selection, but fruit, other than wild cherries or blackberries, was scarce. Many a child found delight in an orange placed in a Christmas stocking.

Because of the railroad, it was possible for settlers to get items they could not produce. The ability to buy these things varied with the success of the crops.

Frederick A. Fleischman came to Kingsbury County, Dakota Territory, about the same time as the Ingallses. His farm is one of twelve

GRASSHOPPERS

Anne Bingham, a cousin of General George Custer's wife, received a good education as well as musical training in New York State. She and her husband, Charles Bingham, settled near Junction City, Kansas, in 1870. Four years later the grasshoppers came.

He kept setting out fruit trees. We had our grapes, our strawberry bed, raspberry vines, and as good a garden as the season would permit. He had to learn how to farm in this climate; when to plant, to sow and to reap. He was fond of experiments, and one year planted peanuts. . . . One year he tried artichokes. . . but the staple crops were winter wheat and corn.

The year 1874 we had a good wheat crop. Our peach trees had come to their first bearing and hung full of fruit. One afternoon in August as I sat sewing I heard a noise on the roof like hailstones. Stepping out I saw the air full of grasshoppers. . . . They got down to business right away. The leaves began falling from the cottonwood shade trees about the house. We saw, too, that our fine peach crop was on the way to destruction. . . . My husband went out to gather them, and I put the washboiler on the stove. . . . I cooked the green peaches, canned them, and they were even nicer than ripe ones. . . . The "hoppers" ate the ones left on the trees down to the pits. Our brother from Washington visited us in November. He broke off some twigs with the stones still hanging on them to take home as evidence, for he said if he told his friends they would call it a "fish story." . . . The sides of the house and the walks were covered with them. They flew like a swarm of bees at one's step. . . . One or two would begin on a melon, . . . and the melon would soon be eaten down to a shell. Onions and beets were a luxury to them, but my husband saved ours, by turning a furrow over them. The corn was destroyed down to the stalk. . . . The grasshoppers stayed so long that they destroyed the newly sowed fields of wheat. . . . We could get mosquito netting at that time. . . . The netting went, like other things, down the throats of the pests. . . . It was difficult even to save the clothes on the line.[10]

listed in the 1880 census. Two years later, after good wheat and oat crops, his account books show that he purchased sugar, tea, flour, fish, coffee, rice, syrup, crackers, and candy. Later, the family celebrated holidays with oysters, cranberries, coconuts, frosted cookies, lemons, grapes, and raisins.

The Fleischmans suffered from the same whims of nature as the other homesteaders. After a few good years for farmers, a prolonged drought set in. It reached its height in 1894, and Fleischman's total income that year was just $95.73. Of that, he spent only $29.72 for groceries and provisions. When lean times came, settlers simply did without.

Chapter Five
SCHOOL DAYS END

For a moment she gathered her courage, then she opened the door and went in. . . .

Streaks of sunshine streamed through the cracks upon a row of six home-made seats and desks that marched down the middle of the room. Beyond them on the studding of the opposite wall, a square of boards had been nailed and painted black, to make a blackboard.

In front of the seats stood a big heating stove. . . . Standing around it were the scholars that Laura must teach. . . . Two boys and one girl were taller than she was. . . .

Laura rapped her pencil on the table. "School will come to order. I will now take your names and ages." . . .

With relief, Laura saw that it was four o'clock. . . .

Laura stood by the window and watched them go. . . .

She cleaned the blackboard, and with the broom, she swept the floor. A dustpan was not needed, the cracks between the floorboard were so wide. She shut the stove's drafts, put on her wraps, took her books and dinner pail, and shutting the door carefully behind her, she set out on her morning path toward Mrs. Brewster's house.

Her first day as a teacher was over.[11]

These Happy Golden Years

Isolation among settlers did not mean a lack of interest in education. Communities had schools, but if one was not close by, mothers used whatever books were available to teach their children at home.

Where schools did exist, attendance was scheduled during periods when children were not needed on the farm. Summer sessions lasted only a few weeks and generally enrolled younger children. Winter sessions might run six weeks to four months, with students up to twenty years of age.

Sometimes the teacher was a man who came to the community seeking the position. In other cases it was a young woman who lived in the community. All were expected to be models of behavior and might be required to sign a document stating that they would not engage in activities, such as card-playing, that might offend those in the community.

Experience was not necessary, nor was a degree from a college. Teachers were certified by appearing before a school committee and proving that they had a basic knowledge of reading, arithmetic, and geography. Laura Ingalls Wilder pointed out that she had never graduated from anything. Even without a high school diploma, she passed the examination that allowed her to teach.

The pay was very low, and the teacher usually boarded at the home of one of the students. For the summer term, which was usually taught by women, pay was $15 to $25 a month. The winter term, taught by both men and women, paid about $10 a month more.

Pupils ranged from very small children just learning to read to students as old as the teacher. Whatever their age, for some it was the first time they had the opportunity to attend school.

Schools were ungraded, and students worked through books like McGuffey's readers, Webster's "blue-back speller," Ray's arithmetic, and Goodrich's history individually. Past the sixth reader (eighth grade), students went into town for school.

Younger children learned by reciting their ABCs and by listening to the older students read their lessons. Some students might have a slate to write on, but work was also done on the blackboard. Paper was too expensive for school lessons.

Recess was a time to work off energy, and boys engaged in rough games while young children enjoyed tag, red rover, hide-and-seek, and blindman's buff. Smaller children played London Bridge is falling down and drop-the-handkerchief. Winter games of chase, like dog-and-deer, were played in circles scraped in the snow.

The school day was shortened on Friday afternoons for competitions such as spelling bees, arithmetic contests, and geography matches. Even adults participated in these.

The schoolhouse, usually painted white, most often was one room with benches for the students and a desk for the teacher. Boards painted black hung on the walls and were wiped clean with a wet cloth. The room was hot in the summer and cold in the winter. Students sitting near the stove might be roasting on one side, while those farther away had chattering teeth.

During winter, different families provided fuel for the stove, but teachers had the responsibility of getting the room warm before the children got there. Then at the close of each day, they swept out the schoolhouse and made it ready for the next day's session. Before they left on cold days, teachers banked the fire by covering red-hot coals with ashes so they would stay hot enough to start the fire the next day. Only then were they free to make their way to the houses where they were staying.

The schoolhouse served as a focal point of the community. Some-times the community church met there. It was also the place for singing schools, spelling schools, scientific societies, and literary groups. Young people particularly enjoyed these courting opportunities.

On the last day of the school, the teacher presented a small gift to each student. Then, as now, students eagerly looked forward to vacation.

Chapter Six
OTHERS CAME FIRST
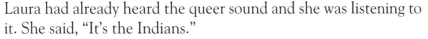

Laura had already heard the queer sound and she was listening to it. She said, "It's the Indians."

Mary's other foot dropped and she stood frozen still. She was scared. Laura was not exactly scared, but that sound made her feel funny. . . . It was something like the sound of an ax chopping, and something like a dog barking, and it was something like a song, but not like any song that Laura had ever heard. It was a wild, fierce sound, but it didn't seem angry. . . .

After Laura was in bed she lay awake a long time. . . . Pa and Ma sat in the firelight and candlelight, reading. . . .

Laura could faintly hear the noise of that wild jamboree in the Indian camp. Sometimes even above the howling of the wind she thought she still heard those fierce yells of jubilation. Faster, faster, faster they made her heart beat. "Hi! Hi! Hi-yi! Hah! Hi! Hah!"[12]

Little House on the Prairie

Settlers moved onto Indian land, often without regard to treaties. By 1830 there had been so much trouble that President Andrew Jackson signed the Indian Removal Act, sending all the tribes west of the Mississippi River. It took ten years and terrible trauma, such as the Cherokee "Trail of Tears," before the removal was completed.

Treaties promised that the prairies and plains would belong to the Indians "as long as the waters run and the grass shall grow." Congress passed a law in 1834 prohibiting anyone from entering Indian lands without permission.

The first wave of intruders were gold miners headed to California. They had no interest in staying on the plains, and early wagon trains did not encounter many problems. As settlers began to establish homes, however, clashes became inevitable.

The American Indians had no concept of owning land. Like air, land was for everyone to use. Plains Indians had no need for fences since they did not raise crops. They followed the buffalo and moved as they needed to.

In trying to keep the settlers and the Indians apart, the government signed treaties that set aside reservations for the different tribes. In 1870, Charles Ingalls's family was among settlers who moved onto the Osage Diminished Reserve, a narrow strip of land in what is today southeast Kansas. The settlers had come upon hearing the news that the

Osage had signed a treaty giving up the territory. But the United States government canceled the treaty when it became known that the purchase price was only 18 cents an acre. Soldiers were sent to remove the settlers, but Charles Ingalls did not wait for them to come. By the time a second treaty opened the land for settlement, the family had left Kansas and returned to Wisconsin.

Because Laura was so young during the time the family lived in Kansas, she relied on things her parents told her in order to fill out her story about living there. Perhaps the sounds they heard were the Osage deliberating the second treaty that paid them $1.25 an acre for their land.

Many frontier families interacted with Indians, sometimes peacefully, sometimes with tragic consequences. One story involved the Parkers, who built a family compound in central Texas in 1835. The following year, eleven-year-old Cynthia Ann Parker, her brother, and two other people were carried off by the Comanches. All others in the compound were killed. During the next twenty-five years, Cynthia Ann forgot her name and everything about her life among white people. Eventually she married a chief. When soldiers killed the chief in a raid in 1860, her teenage son Quanah escaped, but she and her little girl were captured. Soldiers noticed her blue eyes, and after much questioning she remembered her name. She was sent to live with relatives but tried to return to the Comanches. A picture of her with her daughter Topsannah ("Prai-

rie Flower") soon after capture shows her with her hair cut, a Comanche sign of mourning. When Topsannah died, Cynthia Ann lost her will to live. Her son Quanah, however, learned to live in both cultures. A Comanche chief, he became a wealthy livestock owner and a friend of President Theodore Roosevelt.

The Ingallses' encounter with the Osage Indians in Kansas was confined to watching them pass by and feeding those who came to their cabin. In Dakota Territory they met no Indians. Five years before their arrival, General George Custer's soldiers had discovered gold in the Black Hills, land that was sacred to the Lakota Indians. The government was not able to keep gold seekers out, and the Lakota were forced to move.

With settlers arriving in ever-increasing numbers, the government repeated its pattern of treaties that left the Indians with smaller and smaller areas for hunting. The buffalo were gone by 1875, and the Indians could not find food.

Still, they resisted being sent to reservations. Some who were in the northern plains fled to Canada only to return when they could not get enough to eat. The tragic slaughter of defenseless Indians at Wounded Knee, South Dakota, in December 1890, marked the end of the Indians' resistance to entering reservations.

Many of them were taken to Indian Territory (present-day Oklahoma), but before long much of that land was opened for settlement. The Indians got the poor land that the white settlers did not want. In one of the great ironies of history, underneath some of these reservations were rich oil deposits.

Chapter Seven

I AM THE RESURRECTION
AND THE LIFE

"Drink this, little girl."

An arm lifted under her shoulders, and a black hand held a cup to her mouth. Laura swallowed a bitter swallow and tried to turn her head away. . . . "Drink it. It will make you well." . . .

Laura had never seen a black man before and she could not take her eyes off Dr. Tan [sic]. . . . She would have been afraid of him if she had not liked him so much. . . .

Dr. Tan was a doctor with the Indians. He was on his way north to Independence when he came to Pa's house. It was a strange thing that Jack, who hated strangers and never let one come near the house until Pa or Ma told him to, had gone to meet Dr. Tan and begged him to come in.[13]

Little House on the Prairie

Even though settlers were isolated on their farms, there were times for getting together. Neighbors shared the hard work of constructing houses in much the same way as barn raisings were done in the east. Dances were held in them, the dirt floor sprinkled with water to keep down the dust from the jogging feet. Fiddlers played songs such as "Old Dan Tucker" and "Arkansas Traveler" as the square-dance caller sang out for partners to "do-si-do."

As farms grew larger, threshing wheat became a cooperative effort. It was an exciting time for children when the work teams arrived at their farm. Women worked doubly hard to feed the large crew.

The church had a prominent place. If there was only one church building, the congregations took turns using it until they could build a church of their own. Charles Ingalls gave his last three dollars, money intended to buy boots, to help pay for the bell of the Congregational church in Walnut Grove, Minnesota.

There was not enough money to pay a full-time pastor. A Baptist pastor might be a settler himself, but Methodists had a circuit rider who made the rounds to several churches. The Presbyterian and Congregational churches sent missionaries.

Besides the services, church socials and box suppers provided a welcome diversion. There was time for families to visit and young people to get together. The church also provided a link with homes back east. When Ladies Aid Societies in other regions heard about farmers who had no crops and no money after the terrible droughts of 1893–1894, they sent food and clothing to help the families.

Christmas celebrations for the whole community were held either at the church or the schoolhouse. Children's eyes grew wide at the wonder of a tree decorated with strings of popcorn and cherries, and all listened for their names to be called to receive a gift. Family celebrations of the holiday included small, handmade toys and perhaps oranges and white sugar candy placed in a child's stocking on the mantle.

When disaster struck, friends did what they could. Women often nursed sick neighbors, taking small children home with them while their mothers recovered. Broken bones from falls and burns around open fires were common. There was no drugstore to get medicine, and settlers gathered herbs and tree bark to make teas and poultices. Sometimes they had patent medicines that could be bought in town or from a traveling peddler.

Doctors themselves were rare. Dr. George A. Tann, who took care of the Ingallses, was a thirty-four-year-old African-American "eclectic" physician from Pennsylvania. He treated all kinds of ailments. The Tann family, including George's father, who owned 175 acres (70 hectares), is listed right above the Ingalls family on the 1870 census for Montgomery County, Kansas. George, his mother, and a thirteen-year-old servant girl are listed as living in the family. The Tann property, which the doctor inherited on his father's death, adjoined the place where it is assumed the Ingallses lived. Dr. Tann treated Indians for years and became wealthy from oil and real estate investments. He died a respected member of the community at the age of seventy-three, and is buried in Independence, Kansas.

Snakebite, cholera, typhoid fever, malaria, yellow fever, diphtheria—death was a constant companion to homesteaders. Babies had a particularly hard time, as did their mothers. It was not uncommon for mothers to be buried with tiny babies in their arms. Even when the mother lived, children still died at an alarming rate. A family might have ten or twelve children, with only half of them living to adulthood.

Friends rallied around when death struck. In isolated areas, where there was no funeral home and no way to preserve the body, burials were done quickly. Often there was no preacher, and a friend might say some words or read from Scripture at the graveside.

In joy and sorrow, homesteaders supported each other.

PRAIRIE FIRE

O.W. Coursey grew up on a homestead in South Dakota and became a schoolteacher and the author of several books.

One day in April, 1887, when the prairies were dry as gunpowder and when the wind was blowing a regular hurricane from the south, a series of prairie fires sprang up throughout the whole region. Their flames leaped to the skies and swept all before them. . . .

The smoke soon got so dense that it was nearly suffocating the team and myself. I made my way to the far corner of the small field in which I was working, with the team and wagon. In the wagon I had a half barrel of water, covered with a gunny sack, for the team to drink during the day. I climbed into the wagon, jerked the gunny sack covering off the barrel, soused it in the water, wrapped it around my head and shoulders, jumped out and crept under the wagon. . . . The team stuck their heads under the wagon in front of me and kept rubbing their noses against the wet sack, and snorting and pawing viciously.

Finally, when the worst of it was over, I crept out. . . . The team had fared far worse than I had. . . . They were badly singed. . . . I looked toward home and saw my dear mother, astride of Old Jim, our cow pony, coming across the smoking prairie just as hard as the horse could run, to see if her fourteen-year-old boy had perished in the holocaust. . . . Her own hair was awfully singed, and her eyebrows were completely burned off. [14]

Chapter Eight
STORM FRONT

Suddenly there was no sunshine. It went out, as if someone had blown out the sun like a lamp. . . . and at the same moment a wind crashed against the schoolhouse, rattling windows and doors and shaking the walls. . . .

Teacher and all the others were staring at the windows, where nothing but grayness could be seen. . . . Then Miss Garland said, "It is only a storm, children. Go on with your lessons."

There was a loud thumping at the entry. . . .

It opened and a man stumbled in. . . .

"I've come to get you," he told Teacher.

The entry was freezing cold; snow was blowing in between the rough boards of the walls. Laura was chilled before she could snatch her coat and hood from their nail.

"Now, just follow me," said Mr. Foster. . . .

Laura felt that they were going in the wrong direction. She did not know why she felt so. There was nothing to go by—no sun, no sky, no direction in the winds blowing fiercely from all directions. . . .

Then out of the whirling whiteness, something hit her. . . .
She rocked on her feet and stumbled against something solid. . .
. . She had walked against some building. . . .
  It was Mead's Hotel, at the very north end of Main Street.
  Beyond it was nothing but the railroad track covered with snow.
. . . If Laura had been only a few steps nearer the others, they
would all have been lost on the endless prairie north of town.[15]

The Long Winter

No part of the United States has more varied or unpredictable weather
than the plains. Temperatures in North Dakota have been recorded as
high as 121 degrees (50 degrees C) and as low as minus 50 degrees (minus
46 degrees C). The 170-degree variation happens because the land
lies in the middle of the continent, far away from large bodies of water
that moderate temperatures.

In winter, polar air sweeps out of Canada. Snowfall ranges from
about 60 to 100 inches (150 to 250 centimeters) a season, bringing beauty
to the landscape and moisture for crops when it melts.

The snow also poses danger. Blizzards, where the wind seems to
come from every direction, turn the world white. People have died within
a few feet of their houses because they could not see and did not know
where they were. The incident involving the De Smet schoolchildren
was not uncommon. Had Laura not brushed against the hotel, they would
all have died.

The cold is just as dangerous to animals. If left unprotected, livestock freeze where they stand or suffocate when the moisture in their breath freezes in their nostrils. The great storms of 1886–1887 devastated the cattle business.

In summer, warm, moist air moves up from the Gulf of Mexico. It meets cool upper air, and tornadoes begin to churn in "Tornado Alley." Powerful twisters 200 miles (320 kilometers) per hour destroy homes and everything else in their path.

Hailstorms, another result of the two air groups meeting, flatten crops and wipe out a year's work in just minutes.

The area is the windiest place in the country. Wind blowing constantly at 10 to 15 miles (16 to 24 kilometers) per hour affects humans. There are stories of people who were driven crazy by it. Combined with summer heat, it parches crops.

Rainfall is unpredictable on the plains. Sometimes weeks will pass without rain, and then the area may receive in one day most of what it will get for the whole year.

Myths about the weather grew. During the first years the settlers were on the plains, there happened to be an abundance of rainfall, and some believed that the large amount of plowing that had taken place had caused this to happen. Another idea was that energy from railroad tracks and telegraph wires caused rainfall. Some believed that the weather could be permanently changed by planting trees.

     This was not the reason, however, that Congress passed the Timber Culture Act of 1873, which allowed settlers to double their landholdings. This was necessary because 160 acres (65 hectares) in the dry country would not produce enough to feed a family. On the additional land, settlers had to plant 10 acres (4 hectares) of trees and keep them alive for eight years. Almanzo Wilder took his bride, Laura, to a new house on his tree claim.

     A few of these trees have survived. Remnants of them remain scattered in pastures. Sometimes they are seen as stumps or living trees marching in straight lines near a house.

After the early years of abundant rainfall and good crops, normal rainfall returned. This was followed by several years of severe drought. Historically these droughts come in cycles of two to three years, but one that began in the mid-1880s lasted almost ten years. Unless settlers had resources to carry them over, they were forced into debt. With no outside resources, discouraged settlers returned east.

Charles and Caroline Ingalls moved into De Smet and built a house on a lot owned by Caroline. After her husband's death, she and Mary continued to live there. After Caroline's death, Mary spent her last years with her sister Carrie in Rapid City, South Dakota.

Laura and Almanzo Wilder left De Smet. They had lost their home in a fire. Their infant son had died. Successive crops had been destroyed by hail and drought, and their property was heavily mortgaged. Missouri, the "Land of the Big Red Apple," seemed very inviting. After both suffered diphtheria, which left Almanzo crippled, Laura sewed shirts for a dollar a day to earn money to move to Mansfield, Missouri. Laura, Almanzo, and their daughter Rose arrived there on August 31, 1894, with a $100 bill hidden in Laura's writing desk. They bought Rocky Ridge Farm about a mile from town, and it was their home for the next sixty years.

Other settlers remained. Frederick Fleischman, who lived just a few miles to the east of De Smet, spent money only when he had to and suffered through. Ten years after the Ingallses left, Fleischman finally cleared the mortgages from his farm. He had dug a cellar for a new house to accommodate his growing family of nine children, but it took eleven years before he had enough money to complete it. He died in that house in Oldham, South Dakota, in 1929.

Homesteading was intended to be a way for ordinary people to own land so they could provide for their families. Sometimes it seemed to benefit large corporations like the railroads more than the individual people it was intended to help. But this period of history also contains the story of people like Laura Ingalls Wilder and her family. Hers was one of many families who claimed public land in the west—homesteaders who spoke with many different accents, farmers who struggled against natural disasters, settlers who survived loneliness and heartbreak. They persevered, and today the land they settled feeds our nation and its livestock.

NOTES

1. Laura Ingalls Wilder, *By the Shores of Silver Lake* (New York: HarperCollins, 1953), 237. Text copyright 1939 by Laura Ingalls Wilder. Copyright renewed 1967 by Roger L. Macbride.
2. Edwin James, comp., *Account of an Expedition from Pittsburgh to the Rocky Mountains, performed in the Years 1819, 1820 by order of the Hon. J. C. Calhoun, Secretary of War, under the command of Maj. S. J. Long, of the U.S. Top. Engineers* (London: Longman, Hurst, Rees, Orme, and Brown, 1823), vol. 3, 236–237.
3. Lucy Carruth to Fannie Snyder, June 1, 1856. Quoted in *Kansas History: A Journal of the Central Plains*, vol. 9, no. 1 (Spring 1986): 6.
4. Laura Ingalls Wilder, *On the Banks of Plum Creek* (New York: HarperCollins, 1953), 10–11. Text copyright 1937 by Laura Ingalls Wilder. Copyright renewed 1963 by Roger L. Macbride.
5. Howard Ruede, *Sod-House Days: Letters from a Kansas Homesteader 1877–78*, edited by John Ise (New York: Columbia University Press, 1937; Lawrence: University Press of Kansas, 1983), 43.

6. Ibid, 28–29.
7. Wilder, *On the Banks of Plum Creek*, 62.
8. Jacob Dolwig, "From Hungary to North Dakota: An Excerpt from the Diary of Jacob Dolwig," translated from the original by Richard J. Dolwig, *North Dakota Historical Quarterly*, vol. 3, no. 3 (April 1929): 204–208.
9. Laura Ingalls Wilder, *Little Town on the Prairie* (New York: HarperCollins, 1953), 99–100, 104–106. Text copyright 1941 by Laura Ingalls Wilder. Copyright renewed 1969 by Charles F. Lankin, Jr.
10. Anne E. Bingham, "Sixteen Years on a Kansas Farm, 1870–1886," *Collections of the Kansas State Historical Society, 1919–1922*, edited by Will E. Connelley (Topeka: Kansas State Printing Plant, 1923), vol. 15, 515–516.
11. Laura Ingalls Wilder, *These Happy Golden Years* (New York: HarperCollins, 1953), 13, 15, 19–20. Text copyright 1943 by Laura Ingalls Wilder. Copyright renewed 1971 by Roger L. Macbride.
12. Laura Ingalls Wilder, *Little House on the Prairie* (New York: HarperCollins, 1953), 265, 273. Text copyright 1935 by Laura Ingalls Wilder. Copyright renewed 1963 by Roger L. Macbride.
13. Ibid., 190–192.
14. O.W. Coursey, Pioneering in Dakota (Mitchell, SD: Educator Supply Company, n.d.) 68–70.
15. Laura Ingalls Wilder, *The Long Winter* (New York: HarperCollins, 1953), 84, 86–87, 90–91. Text copyright 1940 by Laura Ingalls Wilder. Copyright renewed 1968 by Roger L. Macbride.

INDEX

ABOUT THE AUTHOR

Mary Dodson Wade uses her love of history to create books which reveal the personal side of the times and events she writes about. She holds a master's degree in library science and spent twenty-five years as an elementary school librarian. Now writing full time, she is also a popular speaker at schools and workshops, and serves as regional advisor for the Houston, Texas, chapter of the Society of Children's Book Writers and Illustrators.

Mrs. Wade is the author of *Amelia Earhart: Flying For Adventure*, part of Millbrook's Gateway Biography series, as well as a number of other books, many of them self-published. She lives in Houston.